# 50 Dark Arts Dishes for Home

By: Kelly Johnson

# Table of Contents

- Midnight Truffle Risotto
- Black Garlic and Charcoal-Grilled Ribeye
- Forbidden Forest Wild Mushroom Stew
- Dark Chocolate and Blood Orange Tart
- Smoked Bone Marrow with Black Salt
- Cursed Blackened Cajun Shrimp
- Raven's Feather Squid Ink Pasta
- Alchemist's Black Garlic Soup
- Witch's Brew Charcoal Latte
- Obsidian-Glazed Pork Belly
- Vampire's Delight Red Velvet Cake
- Potion Master's Mulled Wine
- Phantom's Black Sesame Ice Cream
- Dark Spell Braised Short Ribs
- Enchanted Truffle and Black Bean Burger
- Sorcerer's Blackened Chicken
- Hallow's Eve Black Licorice Panna Cotta
- Smoked Beetroot and Goat Cheese Salad
- Shadowy Black Lentil Soup
- Inferno Charcoal-Grilled Octopus
- Moonlit Squid Ink Risotto
- Mystic's Black Rice Pudding
- Blackout Espresso Martini
- Omen's Charred Eggplant Hummus
- Sorcery-Infused Dark Chocolate Mousse
- Black Salt and Honey-Glazed Salmon
- Wicked Spiced Blackberry Cobbler
- Cauldron-Brewed Black Tea Brisket
- Smoldering Bourbon-Glazed Duck
- Black Truffle and Wild Mushroom Tart
- Ashen Fire Roasted Peppers
- Ghostly Dark Cherry Reduction Sauce
- Blackened Lobster with Saffron Butter
- Bewitched Charcoal Lemonade
- Spiced Dark Rum Caramel Tart

- Crypt Keeper's Molasses Baked Beans
- Forbidden Chocolate Chili
- Black Velvet Charcoal Pancakes
- Eldritch Squid Ink Sushi Rolls
- Arcane Spiced Dark Chocolate Truffles
- Necromancer's Roasted Root Vegetables
- Cursed Honey-Glazed Short Ribs
- Haunted Ginger and Black Tea Sorbet
- Smoked Oysters with Black Garlic Butter
- Blackout Espresso and Cardamom Cookies
- Eerie Charcoal-Crusted Rack of Lamb
- Darkened Blackberry and Sage Glaze
- Magician's Black Sesame Macarons
- Bewitched Dark Chocolate Lava Cake
- Nightshade-Infused Blackberry Sangria

# Midnight Truffle Risotto

*A rich, creamy risotto infused with black truffles and midnight decadence.*

**Ingredients:**

- 1 cup Arborio rice
- 4 cups chicken or vegetable broth
- 1/2 cup dry white wine
- 1 small shallot, minced
- 2 tbsp black truffle butter
- 1 tbsp black truffle oil
- 1/2 cup Parmesan cheese, grated
- 1 tsp activated charcoal powder (optional, for a deep black hue)
- Salt & black pepper to taste

**Instructions:**

1. In a saucepan, heat the broth and keep it warm.
2. In a large pan, sauté the shallot in 1 tbsp truffle butter until translucent.
3. Add the Arborio rice and toast for 1-2 minutes.
4. Pour in the white wine and stir until absorbed.
5. Add warm broth one ladle at a time, stirring continuously until the liquid is absorbed before adding more.
6. Once the rice is creamy and tender (about 20 minutes), stir in Parmesan, remaining truffle butter, truffle oil, and charcoal powder.
7. Season with salt and black pepper, then serve hot.

## Black Garlic and Charcoal-Grilled Ribeye

*A smoky, umami-packed steak with deep, mysterious flavors.*

**Ingredients:**

- 2 ribeye steaks
- 4 cloves black garlic, mashed into a paste
- 1 tbsp activated charcoal powder
- 2 tbsp olive oil
- 1 tsp smoked paprika
- 1 tsp sea salt
- 1 tsp black pepper

**Instructions:**

1. Mix black garlic paste, charcoal powder, olive oil, paprika, salt, and black pepper.
2. Coat the steaks with the mixture and let marinate for at least 1 hour.
3. Heat a charcoal grill to high heat.
4. Grill steaks for 3-4 minutes per side for medium-rare, adjusting for desired doneness.
5. Let rest for 5 minutes before slicing.

## Forbidden Forest Wild Mushroom Stew

*A deep, earthy stew featuring wild mushrooms and dark broth.*

**Ingredients:**

- 2 tbsp olive oil
- 1 onion, diced
- 3 cloves garlic, minced
- 2 cups mixed wild mushrooms (shiitake, chanterelle, oyster, etc.)
- 4 cups vegetable broth
- 1 tsp black garlic paste
- 1 tsp dried thyme
- 1 tbsp soy sauce
- 1 tsp activated charcoal powder (optional)
- Salt & pepper to taste

**Instructions:**

1. Heat oil in a pot and sauté onion and garlic until fragrant.
2. Add mushrooms and cook until they release their moisture.
3. Stir in black garlic, soy sauce, thyme, and broth.
4. Simmer for 20 minutes, then blend slightly for a thicker consistency.
5. Stir in charcoal powder and season with salt and pepper.

# Dark Chocolate and Blood Orange Tart

*A rich, bittersweet tart infused with the magic of blood oranges.*

**Ingredients:**

- 1 ½ cups crushed chocolate cookies
- ¼ cup melted butter
- 1 cup dark chocolate (70% or higher), melted
- ½ cup heavy cream
- 1 blood orange, zested and juiced
- 1 tbsp honey
- ½ tsp sea salt

**Instructions:**

1. Mix cookie crumbs with melted butter and press into a tart pan. Chill for 15 minutes.
2. Heat heavy cream, then pour over melted chocolate. Stir until smooth.
3. Stir in blood orange zest, juice, honey, and sea salt.
4. Pour chocolate mixture into the crust and refrigerate until set.

## Smoked Bone Marrow with Black Salt

*Primal decadence served with a smoky, salty twist.*

**Ingredients:**

- 4 beef marrow bones
- 1 tbsp black salt
- 1 tsp smoked paprika
- 1 tsp cracked black pepper
- Fresh bread, for serving

**Instructions:**

1. Preheat the oven to 450°F (232°C).
2. Arrange marrow bones upright on a baking sheet.
3. Sprinkle with black salt, paprika, and black pepper.
4. Roast for 15-20 minutes, until marrow is soft and bubbling.
5. Serve hot with crusty bread.

**Cursed Blackened Cajun Shrimp**

*Spicy, smoky shrimp with a dark Cajun kick.*

**Ingredients:**

- 1 lb shrimp, peeled and deveined
- 1 tbsp olive oil
- 1 tbsp Cajun seasoning
- 1 tsp activated charcoal powder
- 1 tbsp butter
- Lemon wedges for serving

**Instructions:**

1. Toss shrimp with olive oil, Cajun seasoning, and charcoal powder.
2. Heat a skillet over high heat and melt butter.
3. Sear shrimp for 1-2 minutes per side.
4. Serve hot with lemon wedges.

## Raven's Feather Squid Ink Pasta

*A jet-black pasta with the mystery of the deep sea.*

**Ingredients:**

- 1 lb squid ink pasta
- 2 tbsp olive oil
- 3 cloves garlic, minced
- ½ tsp red pepper flakes
- 1 cup cherry tomatoes, halved
- ½ cup white wine
- 1 cup seafood (shrimp, squid, or mussels)
- Salt & pepper to taste

**Instructions:**

1. Cook pasta according to package instructions.
2. In a pan, heat olive oil and sauté garlic and red pepper flakes.
3. Add cherry tomatoes and white wine, simmering until tomatoes soften.
4. Add seafood and cook until just done.
5. Toss with pasta, season with salt and pepper, and serve.

**Alchemist's Black Garlic Soup**

*A rich, dark broth infused with deep umami flavors.*

**Ingredients:**

- 1 head black garlic
- 1 tbsp butter
- 1 onion, sliced
- 4 cups chicken or vegetable broth
- 1 tsp soy sauce
- 1 tsp miso paste
- Salt & pepper to taste

**Instructions:**

1. Melt butter in a pot and sauté onions until caramelized.
2. Add black garlic, broth, soy sauce, and miso paste.
3. Simmer for 20 minutes, then blend until smooth.

**Witch's Brew Charcoal Latte**

*A dark, creamy latte with a hint of mystery.*

**Ingredients:**

- 1 cup milk (or almond/oat milk)
- 1 tsp activated charcoal powder
- 1 tsp honey or maple syrup
- ½ tsp vanilla extract
- ¼ tsp cinnamon

**Instructions:**

1. Heat milk in a saucepan until warm.
2. Whisk in charcoal powder, honey, vanilla, and cinnamon.
3. Froth and serve hot.

**Obsidian-Glazed Pork Belly**

*A lacquered, smoky pork belly with a deep black glaze.*

**Ingredients:**

- 1 lb pork belly
- 2 tbsp soy sauce
- 1 tbsp honey
- 1 tbsp black garlic paste
- 1 tsp activated charcoal powder
- 1 tsp rice vinegar

**Instructions:**

1. Mix soy sauce, honey, black garlic, charcoal powder, and vinegar.
2. Marinate pork belly for 2 hours.
3. Roast at 375°F (190°C) for 40 minutes, basting occasionally.
4. Slice and serve.

# Vampire's Delight Red Velvet Cake

*A deep red, decadent cake fit for the undead.*

**Ingredients:**

**Cake:**

- 2 ½ cups all-purpose flour
- 1 ½ cups sugar
- 1 tsp baking soda
- 1 tsp salt
- 1 tsp cocoa powder
- 1 ½ cups vegetable oil
- 1 cup buttermilk
- 2 large eggs
- 2 tbsp red food coloring
- 1 tsp vanilla extract
- 1 tsp white vinegar

**Frosting:**

- 8 oz cream cheese, softened
- ½ cup unsalted butter, softened
- 2 cups powdered sugar
- 1 tsp vanilla extract

**Instructions:**

1. Preheat oven to 350°F (175°C) and grease two 9-inch cake pans.
2. In a bowl, whisk flour, sugar, baking soda, salt, and cocoa powder.
3. In another bowl, mix oil, buttermilk, eggs, red food coloring, vanilla, and vinegar.
4. Combine wet and dry ingredients, then divide into cake pans.
5. Bake for 30-35 minutes. Let cool.
6. For frosting, beat cream cheese and butter, then mix in sugar and vanilla.
7. Frost the cake and serve!

# Potion Master's Mulled Wine

*A spiced and warming brew to enchant your senses.*

**Ingredients:**

- 1 bottle red wine
- ¼ cup brandy
- ¼ cup honey or sugar
- 1 orange, sliced
- 4 cloves
- 2 cinnamon sticks
- 2 star anise
- ½ tsp black peppercorns

**Instructions:**

1. In a pot, combine all ingredients and heat on low (do not boil).
2. Simmer for 20 minutes, stirring occasionally.
3. Strain and serve warm in goblets.

## Phantom's Black Sesame Ice Cream

*A nutty, velvety black dessert shrouded in mystery.*

**Ingredients:**

- 1 cup black sesame seeds, toasted and ground
- 2 cups heavy cream
- 1 cup whole milk
- ¾ cup sugar
- 4 egg yolks
- ½ tsp vanilla extract

**Instructions:**

1. Heat milk, cream, and sugar in a saucepan until warm.
2. Whisk egg yolks, then slowly pour in warm liquid while whisking.
3. Return to heat and cook until thickened.
4. Stir in black sesame paste and vanilla.
5. Chill, then churn in an ice cream maker.

## Dark Spell Braised Short Ribs

*Fall-off-the-bone ribs in a dark, rich sauce.*

**Ingredients:**

- 4 beef short ribs
- 1 onion, chopped
- 3 cloves garlic, minced
- 2 cups beef broth
- 1 cup red wine
- 1 tbsp soy sauce
- 1 tbsp balsamic vinegar
- 1 tsp smoked paprika
- 1 tsp black pepper

**Instructions:**

1. Brown short ribs in a hot pan, then remove.
2. Sauté onion and garlic until soft.
3. Add wine, broth, soy sauce, vinegar, paprika, and pepper.
4. Return ribs, cover, and simmer for 3 hours.

## Enchanted Truffle and Black Bean Burger

*A magical, umami-packed plant-based burger.*

**Ingredients:**

- 1 can black beans, drained
- ½ cup breadcrumbs
- 1 egg
- 2 tbsp black truffle oil
- ½ tsp smoked paprika
- ½ tsp salt
- ½ tsp black pepper

**Instructions:**

1. Mash black beans, then mix with all ingredients.
2. Form into patties and chill for 30 minutes.
3. Grill or pan-fry until crisp.

# Sorcerer's Blackened Chicken

*A smoky, spiced dish with a darkened crust.*

**Ingredients:**

- 2 chicken breasts
- 1 tbsp paprika
- 1 tsp garlic powder
- 1 tsp onion powder
- ½ tsp cayenne
- ½ tsp black pepper
- ½ tsp salt

**Instructions:**

1. Mix spices and coat chicken.
2. Sear in a hot pan for 3 minutes per side.
3. Finish in a 375°F (190°C) oven for 15 minutes.

# Hallow's Eve Black Licorice Panna Cotta

*A silky, eerie dessert with an anise twist.*

**Ingredients:**

- 2 cups heavy cream
- ½ cup sugar
- 1 tsp anise extract
- 1 tsp activated charcoal powder
- 1 tbsp gelatin
- ¼ cup cold water

**Instructions:**

1. Heat cream and sugar until warm.
2. Sprinkle gelatin over cold water and let bloom.
3. Stir gelatin into warm cream, then add anise and charcoal.
4. Pour into molds and chill.

# Smoked Beetroot and Goat Cheese Salad

*A dark, earthy, and smoky appetizer.*

**Ingredients:**

- 3 beets, roasted and sliced
- ½ cup goat cheese, crumbled
- 2 tbsp balsamic glaze
- 1 tbsp olive oil
- ¼ cup walnuts, toasted

**Instructions:**

1. Arrange beets on a plate.
2. Top with goat cheese and walnuts.
3. Drizzle with balsamic glaze and olive oil.

## Shadowy Black Lentil Soup

*A deep, rich soup with a dark elegance.*

**Ingredients:**

- 1 cup black lentils
- 1 onion, chopped
- 3 cloves garlic, minced
- 4 cups vegetable broth
- 1 tsp cumin
- ½ tsp smoked paprika

**Instructions:**

1. Sauté onion and garlic.
2. Add lentils, broth, and spices.
3. Simmer for 25 minutes.

## Inferno Charcoal-Grilled Octopus

*A fiery, smoky seafood delicacy.*

**Ingredients:**

- 1 octopus, cleaned
- 2 tbsp olive oil
- 1 tbsp lemon juice
- 1 tsp smoked paprika
- ½ tsp salt
- ½ tsp black pepper

**Instructions:**

1. Boil octopus for 45 minutes, then cool.
2. Marinate in oil, lemon juice, paprika, salt, and pepper.
3. Grill over hot charcoal until charred.

# Moonlit Squid Ink Risotto

*A deep, velvety black risotto with an oceanic umami punch.*

**Ingredients:**

- 1 ½ cups Arborio rice
- 4 cups seafood broth
- 1 small onion, finely chopped
- 2 cloves garlic, minced
- ½ cup dry white wine
- 2 tbsp squid ink
- 1 tbsp butter
- ¼ cup Parmesan cheese, grated
- 1 tbsp olive oil
- Salt and black pepper to taste
- Fresh parsley, for garnish

**Instructions:**

1. Heat olive oil in a pan and sauté onion and garlic until translucent.
2. Add Arborio rice and toast for 1-2 minutes.
3. Pour in white wine and let it absorb.
4. Gradually add warm seafood broth, stirring constantly.
5. When rice is tender, stir in squid ink, butter, and Parmesan.
6. Season with salt and pepper, garnish with parsley, and serve hot.

# Mystic's Black Rice Pudding

*A creamy, subtly sweet dessert with a hint of coconut and vanilla.*

**Ingredients:**

- 1 cup black rice
- 2 cups coconut milk
- 1 cup water
- ¼ cup brown sugar
- 1 tsp vanilla extract
- ¼ tsp salt
- Toasted coconut flakes, for garnish

**Instructions:**

1. Rinse black rice and place in a pot with water and coconut milk.
2. Simmer on low heat for 45 minutes, stirring occasionally.
3. Add sugar, salt, and vanilla, stirring until creamy.
4. Serve warm or chilled, topped with coconut flakes.

## Blackout Espresso Martini

*A bold, bittersweet cocktail for late-night revelers.*

**Ingredients:**

- 2 oz vodka
- 1 oz espresso, freshly brewed
- ½ oz coffee liqueur (like Kahlúa)
- ½ oz simple syrup
- Ice cubes
- Black cocoa powder, for garnish

**Instructions:**

1. Shake all ingredients with ice in a cocktail shaker.
2. Strain into a chilled martini glass.
3. Dust with black cocoa powder for an elegant finish.

# Omen's Charred Eggplant Hummus

*A smoky, silky hummus infused with deep flavors.*

**Ingredients:**

- 1 large eggplant
- 1 can chickpeas, drained
- 2 tbsp tahini
- 1 clove garlic
- Juice of 1 lemon
- 2 tbsp olive oil
- ½ tsp smoked paprika
- Salt to taste

**Instructions:**

1. Char the eggplant over an open flame or in the oven until skin is blackened.
2. Scoop out the flesh and blend with chickpeas, tahini, garlic, lemon juice, and olive oil.
3. Add smoked paprika and salt, blend until smooth.

# Sorcery-Infused Dark Chocolate Mousse

*A rich, spellbinding mousse with a silky texture.*

**Ingredients:**

- 6 oz dark chocolate, melted
- 2 tbsp cocoa powder
- 1 cup heavy cream
- 2 egg yolks
- ¼ cup sugar
- ½ tsp vanilla extract

**Instructions:**

1. Heat cream and sugar in a saucepan until warm.
2. Whisk egg yolks and slowly add warm cream while stirring.
3. Mix in melted chocolate, cocoa powder, and vanilla.
4. Chill for at least 2 hours before serving.

# Black Salt and Honey-Glazed Salmon

*A stunning dish with a balance of sweet, salty, and smoky flavors.*

**Ingredients:**

- 2 salmon fillets
- 2 tbsp honey
- 1 tbsp soy sauce
- ½ tsp black salt
- ½ tsp black pepper
- 1 tbsp olive oil

**Instructions:**

1. Whisk honey, soy sauce, and olive oil.
2. Brush over salmon and sprinkle with black salt and pepper.
3. Bake at 375°F (190°C) for 12-15 minutes.

## Wicked Spiced Blackberry Cobbler

*A dark and juicy cobbler bursting with tart-sweet flavor.*

**Ingredients:**

- 3 cups blackberries
- ½ cup sugar
- 1 tsp cinnamon
- ½ tsp nutmeg
- 1 cup flour
- ½ cup butter, melted
- ½ cup milk
- 1 tsp baking powder

**Instructions:**

1. Toss blackberries with sugar and spices, then place in a baking dish.
2. Mix flour, baking powder, butter, and milk, then spread over berries.
3. Bake at 375°F (190°C) for 35 minutes.

# Cauldron-Brewed Black Tea Brisket

*A slow-cooked, tea-infused brisket that melts in your mouth.*

**Ingredients:**

- 3 lbs beef brisket
- 2 cups brewed black tea
- 1 onion, sliced
- 3 cloves garlic, minced
- 1 tbsp Worcestershire sauce
- 1 tbsp soy sauce
- ½ tsp black pepper

**Instructions:**

1. Sear brisket in a hot pan.
2. Place in a slow cooker with black tea, onion, garlic, Worcestershire, and soy sauce.
3. Cook on low for 6-8 hours.

## Smoldering Bourbon-Glazed Duck

*A bold, rich duck dish with a caramelized bourbon glaze.*

**Ingredients:**

- 2 duck breasts
- ½ cup bourbon
- ¼ cup maple syrup
- 1 tbsp soy sauce
- ½ tsp black pepper
- 1 tbsp butter

**Instructions:**

1. Sear duck breasts skin-side down until crispy.
2. Remove excess fat, then glaze with bourbon, syrup, soy sauce, and black pepper.
3. Cook for 5 more minutes, then let rest before slicing.

# Black Truffle and Wild Mushroom Tart

*A decadent, umami-rich tart with earthy flavors.*

**Ingredients:**

- 1 sheet puff pastry
- 1 cup wild mushrooms, sliced
- 2 tbsp black truffle oil
- ½ cup Gruyère cheese, shredded
- ½ cup heavy cream
- 1 egg
- Salt and black pepper

**Instructions:**

1. Preheat oven to 375°F (190°C).
2. Sauté mushrooms in truffle oil.
3. Mix heavy cream, egg, salt, and pepper, then fold in mushrooms.
4. Pour into pastry and bake for 25 minutes.

## Ashen Fire Roasted Peppers

*A smoky, slightly charred pepper dish with deep flavors.*

**Ingredients:**

- 4 bell peppers (red, yellow, or orange)
- 2 tbsp olive oil
- 1 tsp smoked paprika
- ½ tsp sea salt
- ½ tsp black pepper
- 1 clove garlic, minced

**Instructions:**

1. Place whole bell peppers directly over an open flame or under the broiler until blackened.
2. Let them cool, then peel off the charred skin.
3. Slice into strips and toss with olive oil, smoked paprika, salt, pepper, and garlic.

# Ghostly Dark Cherry Reduction Sauce

*A hauntingly rich and tart sauce perfect for meats and desserts.*

**Ingredients:**

- 2 cups dark cherries, pitted
- ½ cup balsamic vinegar
- ¼ cup brown sugar
- 1 tsp black pepper
- ½ tsp salt

**Instructions:**

1. Simmer all ingredients in a saucepan over medium heat until thickened (about 15 minutes).
2. Blend until smooth and serve over meats or desserts.

# Blackened Lobster with Saffron Butter

*A luxurious, smoky lobster dish infused with golden saffron butter.*

**Ingredients:**

- 2 lobster tails
- 2 tbsp butter
- 1 pinch saffron threads
- 1 tsp smoked paprika
- ½ tsp black pepper
- ½ tsp sea salt

**Instructions:**

1. Melt butter and steep saffron threads for 5 minutes.
2. Season lobster tails with paprika, salt, and pepper.
3. Grill over high heat until slightly blackened, then brush with saffron butter before serving.

## Bewitched Charcoal Lemonade

*A mysterious, jet-black lemonade with a hint of citrus magic.*

**Ingredients:**

- 4 cups water
- ½ cup fresh lemon juice
- ¼ cup honey or agave syrup
- ½ tsp activated charcoal powder
- Ice cubes

**Instructions:**

1. Mix all ingredients in a pitcher and stir well.
2. Serve over ice and watch the magic unfold!

## Spiced Dark Rum Caramel Tart

*A sinfully rich caramel tart with a spiced dark rum twist.*

**Ingredients:**

- 1 pie crust
- 1 cup brown sugar
- ½ cup butter
- ¼ cup dark rum
- ½ cup heavy cream
- ½ tsp cinnamon

**Instructions:**

1. Pre-bake the pie crust at 350°F (175°C).
2. Melt butter and sugar in a saucepan, stirring until golden.
3. Add rum, cream, and cinnamon, cooking until thick.
4. Pour into crust and chill before serving.

# Crypt Keeper's Molasses Baked Beans

*A deep, dark, and smoky twist on classic baked beans.*

**Ingredients:**

- 2 cups cooked black beans
- ¼ cup molasses
- 2 tbsp brown sugar
- 1 tbsp smoked paprika
- 1 tsp black pepper
- 1 clove garlic, minced

**Instructions:**

1. Mix all ingredients in a slow cooker or pot.
2. Simmer on low heat for 1-2 hours until flavors meld.

## Forbidden Chocolate Chili

*A dangerously rich and spicy chili with a touch of dark chocolate.*

**Ingredients:**

- 1 lb ground beef
- 1 onion, chopped
- 1 can diced tomatoes
- 2 cups black beans
- 1 tbsp chili powder
- ½ tsp cinnamon
- 1 oz dark chocolate, chopped

**Instructions:**

1. Sauté beef and onion until browned.
2. Add tomatoes, beans, chili powder, and cinnamon.
3. Simmer for 30 minutes, then stir in dark chocolate before serving.

# Black Velvet Charcoal Pancakes

*Fluffy, dramatic pancakes with a deep black hue.*

**Ingredients:**

- 1 cup flour
- 1 tbsp activated charcoal powder
- 1 tbsp cocoa powder
- 1 tsp baking powder
- 1 egg
- ¾ cup milk
- 1 tbsp sugar

**Instructions:**

1. Whisk dry ingredients together.
2. Mix in egg and milk until smooth.
3. Cook pancakes in a buttered pan until fluffy and dark.

# Eldritch Squid Ink Sushi Rolls

*A stunning and eerie black sushi roll with oceanic flavors.*

**Ingredients:**

- 1 cup sushi rice
- 1 tbsp rice vinegar
- 1 tsp sugar
- ½ tsp salt
- 1 tsp squid ink
- 4 sheets nori (seaweed)
- ½ cucumber, sliced
- ½ avocado, sliced
- 4 oz raw tuna or salmon

**Instructions:**

1. Cook rice and mix with vinegar, sugar, salt, and squid ink.
2. Spread rice on nori, then add fillings.
3. Roll tightly, slice, and serve with soy sauce.

## Arcane Spiced Dark Chocolate Truffles

*Rich, spiced chocolate truffles with a magical depth of flavor.*

**Ingredients:**

- 8 oz dark chocolate, chopped
- ½ cup heavy cream
- ½ tsp cinnamon
- ¼ tsp cayenne pepper
- Cocoa powder, for coating

**Instructions:**

1. Heat cream and pour over chocolate, stirring until smooth.
2. Mix in spices and chill until firm.
3. Roll into balls and coat with cocoa powder.

## Necromancer's Roasted Root Vegetables

*A smoky, caramelized blend of dark, earthy flavors.*

**Ingredients:**

- 1 sweet potato, cubed
- 1 beet, cubed
- 1 parsnip, sliced
- 2 tbsp olive oil
- 1 tsp smoked paprika
- ½ tsp black salt

**Instructions:**

1. Toss vegetables with oil, paprika, and salt.
2. Roast at 400°F (200°C) for 30 minutes until caramelized.

## Cursed Honey-Glazed Short Ribs

*Slow-cooked, fall-off-the-bone short ribs with a hauntingly rich honey glaze.*

**Ingredients:**

- 4 lbs beef short ribs
- ½ cup honey
- ¼ cup soy sauce
- 2 tbsp balsamic vinegar
- 1 tbsp black garlic paste
- 1 tsp smoked paprika
- ½ tsp black pepper
- 1 tsp salt

**Instructions:**

1. Preheat oven to 325°F (163°C).
2. Mix honey, soy sauce, vinegar, garlic paste, paprika, and pepper.
3. Sear short ribs in a pan, then coat with glaze.
4. Bake for 2.5-3 hours, basting occasionally, until tender.

# Haunted Ginger and Black Tea Sorbet

*A ghostly, refreshing sorbet with deep black tea and a spicy ginger kick.*

**Ingredients:**

- 2 cups brewed black tea (strong)
- ½ cup sugar
- 1 tbsp grated fresh ginger
- ½ cup lemon juice
- ¼ cup honey
- ½ tsp activated charcoal (optional, for color)

**Instructions:**

1. Simmer tea, sugar, and ginger until sugar dissolves.
2. Strain, then mix with lemon juice, honey, and charcoal.
3. Freeze, stirring every 30 minutes, until sorbet-like.

## Smoked Oysters with Black Garlic Butter

*A luxurious smoky appetizer with rich, umami-laden black garlic butter.*

**Ingredients:**

- 12 fresh oysters, shucked
- 4 tbsp butter, softened
- 2 cloves black garlic, mashed
- ½ tsp smoked paprika
- ½ tsp sea salt

**Instructions:**

1. Mix butter, black garlic, paprika, and salt.
2. Spoon onto each oyster and smoke on a grill for 5-7 minutes.

## Blackout Espresso and Cardamom Cookies

*Deep, dark, and intensely rich cookies with a hint of exotic spice.*

**Ingredients:**

- 1 cup flour
- ½ cup cocoa powder
- 1 tbsp espresso powder
- ½ tsp ground cardamom
- ½ tsp baking soda
- ½ cup butter, softened
- ½ cup brown sugar
- 1 egg

**Instructions:**

1. Preheat oven to 350°F (175°C).
2. Cream butter and sugar, then mix in egg.
3. Stir in dry ingredients and form dough balls.
4. Bake for 10-12 minutes.

# Eerie Charcoal-Crusted Rack of Lamb

*A strikingly dark crust with smoky, earthy depth.*

**Ingredients:**

- 1 rack of lamb
- 2 tbsp activated charcoal powder
- 2 tbsp Dijon mustard
- 1 tbsp rosemary, chopped
- 1 tsp black pepper
- 1 tsp sea salt

**Instructions:**

1. Preheat oven to 400°F (200°C).
2. Coat lamb with mustard, then press charcoal, rosemary, salt, and pepper onto it.
3. Roast for 25-30 minutes.

## Darkened Blackberry and Sage Glaze

*A bold, sweet-savory glaze for meats or desserts.*

**Ingredients:**

- 1 cup blackberries
- ¼ cup balsamic vinegar
- 2 tbsp honey
- 1 tsp fresh sage, chopped
- ½ tsp black pepper

**Instructions:**

1. Simmer all ingredients until thickened.
2. Strain and use as a glaze for meats or desserts.

## Magician's Black Sesame Macarons

*A delicate and nutty macaron with a mysterious twist.*

### Ingredients:

- 1 cup almond flour
- 1 cup powdered sugar
- 2 tbsp black sesame powder
- 2 egg whites
- ¼ cup sugar

### Filling:

- ½ cup butter, softened
- ¼ cup black sesame paste
- ½ cup powdered sugar

### Instructions:

1. Sift almond flour, powdered sugar, and sesame powder.
2. Whip egg whites, gradually adding sugar until stiff peaks form.
3. Fold in dry ingredients, pipe circles, and let rest for 30 minutes.
4. Bake at 300°F (150°C) for 12-15 minutes.
5. Mix filling ingredients and sandwich between macarons.

## Bewitched Dark Chocolate Lava Cake

*A spellbindingly rich dessert with a molten chocolate center.*

**Ingredients:**

- ½ cup dark chocolate
- ¼ cup butter
- ¼ cup sugar
- 1 egg + 1 egg yolk
- ¼ cup flour

**Instructions:**

1. Preheat oven to 425°F (220°C).
2. Melt chocolate and butter together.
3. Whisk in sugar, eggs, and flour.
4. Pour into ramekins and bake for 10-12 minutes.

## Nightshade-Infused Blackberry Sangria

*A dark, fruity, and spiced sangria for an enchanted evening.*

**Ingredients:**

- 1 bottle red wine
- ½ cup brandy
- ½ cup blackberries
- ¼ cup black currants
- 1 cinnamon stick
- 1 tbsp honey

**Instructions:**

1. Mix all ingredients and let sit for at least 2 hours.
2. Serve chilled over ice.